Halos for Heroes, Friends & A Few People I Don't Like

A Poetry Collection

Khadijah Z. Ali-Coleman

DEDICATION

Dedicated to my dear friend Tinu Abayomi-Paul, who passed away in September 2023 in the midst of being a disability activist living with cancer and long COVID-19. May her name and contributions to the world always be remembered.

ABOUT THE AUTHOR

Khadijah Z. Ali-Coleman, Ed.D., is a mother, community organizer, and cultural architect with over 20 years of applied experience transforming places into arts and educational spaces. She is award-winning performance artist Khadijah Moon and a multi-genre writer who is a playwright and filmmaker. She served as the second Poet Laureate of Prince George's County, Maryland, from 2023 to 2025.

Dr. Ali-Coleman is the author of the poetry collections *A Park Stands On All of Our Graves* (2025), *For the Girls Who Do Too Much* (2024), and *The Summoning of Black Joy* (2023); the children's book *Mariah's Maracas* (2018); and co-editor of the book *Homeschooling Black Children in the US: Theory, Practice and Popular Culture* (2022).

Dr. Ali-Coleman is the founding director of **Black Writers for Peace and Social Justice**, a 501(c)(3) nonprofit started in 2024. She founded the multidisciplinary arts group **Liberated Muse** in 2008 and co-founded the national education research group, **Black Family Homeschool Educators and Scholars, LLC (BFHES)**, in 2020, in the midst of the COVID-19 quarantine. BFHES has provided a supportive space for over 3000 families since then, offering annual teach-ins and workshops.

She lives in Baltimore, Maryland, with her family.

Praise for *A Park Stands on All of Our Graves*

Khadijah Z. Ali-Coleman's poems explore themes of identity, resistance, social justice, history, culture, and the American machine's cringeworthy hypocrisy. She tenderly examines the political trends/winds with a raw, soulful verse, which begs to be heard. This collection is a unique form of militant jazz. A must read.

-Synnika A. Lofton, author of *Monsters in My Head*

Both a meal and a treasure trove of lessons, A Park Stands On All of Our Graves is something to chew on, savor, and swallow...Dr. Ali-Coleman's latest offering, is a dish best served simmering and without an iota of an apology.

-B. Sharise Moore, author and poetry editor of *FIYAH Magazine*

A Park Stands on All Our Graves is the rough root medicine we need for what ails us in these menacing times.

-Derrick Weston Brown, author of *Wisdom Teeth and On All Fronts; Floodgates Poetry Series Vol.5*

This new poetry collection from Khadijah Ali-Coleman seizes our national crisis and dares to talk back to it...Khadijah Z. Ali-Coleman is a voice for our time.

-V. Melissa Holland, Ph.D., City of Laurel Arts Council, Prince George's County Arts & Humanities Council

A Park Stands on All of Our Graves is a fierce lament against racism's violence wherever it raises its demon-like head in the world.

- Truth Thomas, Inaugural Poet Laureate of Howard County, MD

ACKNOWLEDGMENTS

This poetry collection was published and marketed thanks to a grant from the Prince George's Arts and Humanities Council (PGAHC) Artist Fellowship Grant. I also worked with them as the Poet Laureate of Prince George's County, MD, before moving to Baltimore, MD. It was through this work as poet laureate that I met Dr. V. Melissa Holland, one of the board members of PGAHC, who has invited me or recommended me for public poetry events and public school visits where I was able to witness the powerful impact of poetry on young people. I am very proud of the students in Ms. Angellita Dillon's class at Laurel High School, in particular, for putting together their own poetry collection after my visit during National Poetry Month in 2025. What an awesome feat! The poem "Who are you when no one is watching" was written as a writing prompt for them when I facilitated my workshop with them.

I would also like to thank the John F. Kennedy Center for the Performing Arts Social Impact team, who booked me and my performance group, Liberated Muse, from 2017 to 2025 to present a myriad of offerings, including shows on the Millennium Stage where some of the poems in this collection were first shared. I also thank the University of Maryland, Baltimore County (UMBC), my alma mater, that invited me to present the Winter 2024 commencement speech. I included in this collection the poem I presented during my speech.

Thank you to all of the readers who chose to pick up this book today and give it a read-through. I appreciate you and send you my best. I encourage you to give thanks for your loved ones.

Khadijah Z. Ali-Coleman

TABLE OF CONTENTS

PART III:
Affirmations & Toasts To and From the Ancestors   71

"I have known the joy and pain of friendship. I have served and been served. I have made some good enemies for which I am not a bit sorry. I have loved unselfishly, and I have fondled hatred with the red-hot tongs of Hell. That's living."

— Zora Neale Hurston

PART I:

Halos for Heroes, Friends & A Few People (and Things) I Don't Like

The Final Days of Walking Earth and Rising Sun

you out here
trying to sell
dreams to people
sipping on nightmares
for nourishment

them who find
pleasure in
the discards
of lesser men.
They ain't
your people.

You are soaring
eagle, latchkey kid
with growing
responsibilities.
You lift heavy
with graceful
unawareness of
hopelessness.

you forget
disappointment
long enough
to plant mercy,
clasping
hands that pray.

raining hands
sprinkling
hope on seeds,
covering sacred
soil. this act
is praise
song. is suicide.

is a suicider's guide
to following
the light
they ignored. an
unending work,
this living
as both earth,
and sun, living as
gardener & scourge,
feeding mouths
that always finagle
the last morsel.
tongues that twitch

baiting
and switching
and lying
proudly. promising
falling water
during unseasonal
drought. they ain't
your people.

you

forget blare
and bolster.
your language is
cashmere and
silk. ceasing motion
of a building storm.
your presence
brings a washing,
clean of their
bruising presence.

finally.
you are
golden again,
shaking bluster
from wings
barely singed
by wind.
ready to fly
Home

A Poem for Candace Turning 40

There will be moths who eat away at your old things
and force you to be new. You will recoil at first before
finding the fit comfortable. Familiar is not safety

these days. Home lives within this swirling freshness.
Your mouth circles *no* with firmness and a confidence
shrunken in shadows before. Girl, you get louder

without realizing it! Finally you will hear yourself
greeting their astonished eyes. And, you will fall in love
with this sound. You can fit your whole self– with

room to man-spread–into new spaces that softly
delight! Your arms will live to raise high towards the sky
in these spaces. Let them. Your mind is unlearning

confinement and recalibrating. At this nexus, you no
longer swallow diversion so easily. Instead, you say all
the things that thinged in silence before. You shed

subtext as life jacket, for, this loosened tongue is feral
when unleashed, straightening ties in dizzying haste.
But, oh, how sweet the taste of honesty!

We Be Jazz (Liberated Muse)

Liberated muse is
woman,
is Black,
is poetry. Is
grandmother's blessing
&auntie's Christmas check
you didn't expect. Is
laughing so hard
you cryin'.

Liberated Muse is
the smell
of something good
to eat, curry chicken
bubbling in the pot,
ocean waves lulling
you calm. We be jazz
on Sunday and 90's R & B
on a Monday.

Liberated Muse is
red, black and green,
casual Fridays
&ball gowns
the rest of the week.
We are mermaids
& butterflies, and
the spirit of Zora
&Harriet. We is all this.

Yellow Halos

We are chamomile
&yellow
halos
Cuz lucky
falls from our
lips&
pays high rent
to stand
on these streets
as we wail tunes
into tomorrow
that follow us back
into today
You teach me
how to breathe
under water
as I float
while standing, rising air
I help you remember
  yourself
as soft and brave
count your laps
around the sun
as we dance
 and swim
between stars,
I call you softly
to plant a garden
in your hand

so that you
may carry
your flowers
with you forever,
unblemished
by dust

Because of Black Women

i doubt myself
&love myself

believe that
all things are possible

&bitches ain't shit
because my mother

loved me and hated me
sold me out because she could

chased that boy
who threw a rock at me

but still ain't rock
with me when i got grown

and all the friends
who ain't never had my back

still fucked with me
on Saturdays sometimes

so i don't have a problem
with all Black women

and the ones i do have one with
ain't been a problem all the time

but I think it is safe to say
ain't no one awful all the time

and ain't no one great
all the time, except me, maybe

because i am a Black woman
and I love me some me

The Fantastic Smile

Give thanks

for early shade, before coffee,
that "hm" and eye roll,

Hard sucking of teeth when
a person you know was talking

about you last week has the nerve to walk by.
The fantastic smile you broadly wear

when she turns around and
you stare her down until

she turns back around.
Let's give thanks for this quiet act of violence.

Carry this warrior weapon
for every sharp place you may enter,

where crafty critters post up
and angle their heads, whispering.

Give thanks

for car notes and mortgages
that staple your arms

to your side, reminders

of adult duties.

Catching a charge is for the untethered.
Those who lack vision.

Honestly, though, you too old
to beat an old woman's ass.

You an old woman, too.

You can't be laying hands
on everyone who finds

your name too delicious
to keep out their mouth.

Give thanks for the gossipers,
them messy Tinas who never learned

that competition is a man's
game with no winner.

They are accidental fans,
booster of a brand

you didn't even know
you were advertising.

Smile on, brand ambassador.
Swish and float, and saturate

the space with your glow.
Surely, you know the sun burns?

A Typical Poem About Menopause

You are so hot!
Rolling tears of perspiration
pool in the valleys
underneath each eye. Your

hair curls along the
edges of your forehead,
recoiling from the stinging
heat that refuels itself

mercilessly. A livid bonfire,
waving red and orange
flags feeds off of
your unspoken furies. All

the no's! and nevers
you swallowed while weeping
live within the walls
of a depleted uterus

wearing dark glasses and
smoking a cigarette, packing
for retirement. How can
your skin be creamy

silk on Monday and
the scratchiness of parchment
by noon on Wednesday?
Stories woven within each

freckle laugh and cry
in commiseration. Water forgets
its job to extinguish
this unwavering furnace. It

knows the history you've
suppressed to survive. Your
bones tell fortunes now,
predicting rain. The knees'

creaks and groans are
now your second language.
Tomorrow, will you remember
to smile in the morning?

A Poem for Colie

it's like you
hear my tears
falling, even
when you aren't
nearby, even when
you are asleep&
in another day&
i am still in
sunday

you are always
listening to my
heart& sometimes
i don't have
the words to
say thank you
for seeing me
&being my friend
because

i sometimes don't
believe that this
is real& because
some friends are
only shadows disappearing
but I know you
are real because
you are here
still, before&   after the sun

A Praisesong for Goals

(a poem for Lyn)

give thanks
for friends
with suns
in earth signs
who speak
with dependable
tongues
&generous hearts
friends who
are easily
intelligent
but choose
silly days
with us
to drink
&dance

you asked us
what our goals were
for 2025
&we laughed
&laughed because
even while drinking
you are
worried about
our future
&because
you were just

trying to start
a conversation
five past midnight
even after four
glasses of wine&
a carefully poured
brown liquor
concoction,
here you are,
still the
most lucid of us all

A Poem for Angie

tucked deeply
in this poem
is a stocked future
not dependent
on your depletion,
a thank you
sent in advance

this poem sends
blessings that
taste like chocolate
&remembers birthdays
without a
Facebook reminder

in this poem
i place ocean
&sailboat
&cooling breeze
carrying a
sleepy lullaby
to lull you

there is much to be said
about the devoted,
the daughters
who parent
their parents
&angle themselves

90 degrees
always, pouring
into others
without pause,
never flagging

but what is
rarely said
is thank you
or rest now
or no thank you,
i am good
so, for that,
i send this poem

reminding you
that you are
more than enough
&always too good
for the moments
that flood
your minutes

Tinu in Technicolor

Today you are 19 years old and alive
And breathing and your body is a fortress
that is not broken by cancer because you are
19 and barely aware of the peril of aging. Youth is
forever.

Carefree is a verb. Daytime is only a necessary
nuisance bridging In and out, to and fro. It is all a
mirage and still we are seeking its solid offering. These
knees bend easily. These college classes
leak tedious distraction from the lilt of
random lovers weaving in and out of view.

Oh, god!

Your stories can wake the sleeping!
The inevitable laughing always kissed the rafters. Your
saucer-wide eyes tell the most. Oh, Queen of TMI, you
never skipped the nasty parts. Your details included
each crevice and bump on his ____.

I was always traumatized and amazed
by the stunning attention to specifics. You saw violet,
aqua and turquoise when sometimes there was only
Blue. The stories that lived within your body were
always stronger than the scourge that destroyed it.
Your death stares dully at this empty space that
whines

an ugly beige in your absence

The Language
*a performance and prayer remembering Toni
Morrison*

She curves lips,
Rounding Os in elegance

Shaped wide and heavy
Holding your mouth full

Your brain widening
Long legged audacity

Fire in belly blaze
Lit

SHE Hollers consonants
Whispering crescendos

Into poetic prose like teardrops
Dripping the pain of the voiceless

Ancestors she remembers
Her language is the finest of all

Draping the pages into immaculate
Landscapes

that dip heavy into
The blood-filled canyons

into the graves of the enslaved
Into the riches of the ditches dug deep

To imprison us
She sets us free

Her language is the dialect of the wise women
The clucking chatter of the common folk

The regal vanity of the few who knew
That the language is the nectar of the journey

The soil of the garden that is
the growing page

And like a good mother
She birthed this knowing in us

For
always

(closing prayer)

Master artist
Queen of language and literature
Memory of history, culture and creation

We call your name into the silence

blanketing the room with the brilliance of your light
rivaling the luster of the star Sirius
sparkling so bright we are left breathless in its sheen
even in death, your light still gleams
you are teacher and goddess mother,
wielding language as your golden specter
impeccable perfection

each word placed spectacularly
in monumental resurrection of the word
gilded gold
in each line our story is told
Pecola, Sula, Nell, Pilate, Sethe, Denver, Baby Suggs
Living, breathing, full-bodied people

Your pen breathed life into each woman
Dressing them In your vivid fluency
Your mesmerizing imagination
beautifully realized
Shared gracefully with the world
This tribute is for you
We are better because of your gallant appreciation
and care with our fragile remembering
ushering us gently toward a better understanding of
who we are

This word, this moment, this fraction of infinity is for
Chloe Ardelia Wofford
For our Toni Morrison
With love, always

D'Angelo Returns to Source

The names have been changed to protect those who may not be drama queens any more and may have careers that require them to hide their edge. Names may also be changed because I am over 50 and some of the details aren't as clear. But, I still remember your voice and when I first heard it.

It's 1995 and I have graduated from college in May, but I am still popping up on campus to see my friends who haven't graduated yet. It hasn't sunk in that I am an alumna yet, and I miss my routines. I miss my friends. Especially my friend, Keisha. She is my bougie-ghetto friend who got in a fight for me that time last summer when we had a summer fellowship together in Wisconsin at that university near the river. She had my back when that crazy girl Robyn bit me over a man. College is a wild place.

I will be starting graduate school that fall and looking for a summer job as I chat it up with the person at the front desk who lets me into the residence hall without leaving my ID. I used to work as a desk attendant. They know me. I don't remember what we talked about. I don't remember who was working the desk. What I do remember is hearing your voice when Keisha opened her dorm room door to let me in.

Whatever the male equivalent of sultriness is is what you sound like. Chill sexy low growl. Arousing harmonies over bass melting into the tinkling of piano key notes. Floating. I am self-conscious.

"Who is this?"

Keisha says your name: D'Angelo. Shoving your CD in my hand absently, she prattles on about her boyfriend's trifling ass while she gets dressed to meet him.

Do do doot do doot do dododooo
"Baby, let's cruise awayyy from here"

I am tempted to tuck Keisha's copy of your CD in my purse to take back to my shared apartment. But, I don't carry a purse at this time. I also don't have a working CD player right now.

In your leather jacket and braids, you look like the kind of man I had not known yet. Curiosity quickens my interest, hands turning the case over and over again

"D'Angelo," I said aloud.

"Never heard of him."

Who Are You When No One is Watching?

(a writing prompt for students in Ms.Dillon's class at 3pm)

Are you sneaky?
Are you wild?
Are you spicy?
Are you mild?
Are you truth?
Or all lies?
Are you a giver?
Are you the prize?
Do you waver?
Or do you stand firm?
Are you brave or
Do you squirm?
Are you a watcher
Or do you do?
Can others say
They can depend on you?
Do you help
Or do you leave?
Are you mean
Or easy to please?
What is your pleasure?
What is your pain?
Do you repeat
Or do you refrain?
Can you truly say
You are glad about you
Do you believe who you are
true blue?
Or are you a reflection
And not authenticity
Who exactly is it
you are trying to be?

Ode to Jamia &her wicked sense of self

I pencil in Black lines to form edges where there are
none
Some say edgy is a good thing, so I'm gon go head
&draw me some
  Tilt my linear to form sharp circles that peak& point
         &sometimes bend
  Creating something that is no longer a circle, unique
        from center to the very end
If I could fake what is considered normal &for a little
while experience quiet
I would trade in a bit of this which bubbles in queer
regions &put myself on a strict diet
 --> but only for a second; cause the straight & narrow
         ain't always clear
Purple stains blot locked hearts& brains when they
refuse to feel &hear
   As I smudge the edge a bit, I add the color and it
        begins to blend
  until no longer there is a boundary between where
       there is end and I begin

A World in Sudden Dark

(For Nikki Giovannii)

not empty, only quiet
with the occasional buzz
and chirp of life that does not grieve
does know that Truth has lost
a soldier in a world that has become stony
silence bearing the brunt of mercy

there will be no foot fall,
no easy pressing of boundaries,
no spilling of cordial banter as
the left unsaid
prance in their hurry, cause there

will be no call out tonight,
only closed mouths
and deep thoughts one gets
when one is close reading,
cause when a poet dies,
there is lots of reading

and remembering and claiming
to be kin with a person
you only know through their
pen prints on a page
retooled for consumption
and repurposed for memorial

To All the Books I Buy and Have Not Read Yet

i get you
I know
how it feels
to be wanted
&then ignored
&forgotten
when you have finally been gotten.   ain't it funny
how interest wanes
so quickly
after the rabid chase
has been won?
you are still
interesting
&beautiful
&full of soooo
much more
than the mystery
that brought you
here. &even if
you are never
picked up again
or opened carefully
with an interest
that seems that
it will last forever, you will
always be Incandescent
specialness &wanted
for what is on

the inside   &just because

Praisesong for the Black Woman Who Publishes Herself

If Charlotte Osgood Mason hadn't tossed money for
Black tales, what literature highlights of the Harlem

Renaissance would we know today? Would
Gwendolyn Brooks' name fall so easily from our lips if

Richard Wright hadn't made the call to his publishing
co. to publish her work? How long will culture bandits

in suits and ties continue to wage war over first rights
for financial access to our creative outputs? The

question leads me to ask about the legitimacy of my
own writerly presence within this creative ecosystem

if I want to, dare I say, own my own art. Am I really a
writer if I claim my words by purchasing the ISBN,

and handing my book to each person who wants to
read it? Does that count? If I cried each word and

glued it to the page with each reluctant lick, does that
mean that I can legitimately say that I am, in some

way, somehow, a writer? Even if there is no contract
with my signature signing over my rights to my

creative and digital intellectual property? If my

audio is read with my own voice and a lawyer is not

negotiating adaptation plans between the publisher
and production company who live in the same house,

will I get to submit my book for award consideration or
get my opportunity for tenure at the university that

deems me worthy to teach but is kinda iffy on
ensuring me job security? Does it count if I

experienced the story that found its way to the page
through a failed suicide attempt, a miscarriage, two

abortions, beer pockets and Riesling dreams, wearing
a dashiki and an African name given to me

from a father raised on drugs and jail? I can still
pronounce big words and drop vowels on command.

But, does it count if I'm not on a list that shows what
sells best or makes white folks chatter and gather

and feel seen and a part of the action? Am I a writer if
I write for myself and publish for myself and only

hope that one day my great-grandchild who I may
never meet gets a chance to know what their

great-grandma really thinks and wishes she was still
around to read this book out loud? Does this poem

count? Do these words count? Is this ending the last
word? What counts and will really make me be
considered a real writer and my work legitimately part
of a canon that powders its pink nose with the fumes

of my labor? If a white patron has not plucked me
from the proverbial cotton field for a gig in the big

house, should I sit on my hands until one comes along?
Does the shiny book cover that I just

designed brightly in red, white and blue warrant a
look? If Wheatley were not so remarkable in her

determination to write when it was illegal for her to
read, would we even know her name? Perhaps we

would. Most likely, we would not. The dropping of coins
fetched by her talent clink in her mistress'

coffers as her death at 31 followed a failed attempt to
publish on her own. Maybe it is time to admit that we

would not know the names of Langston, Zora, Toni nor
Alice if they were not sponsored by the villains

renamed in their stories. We have greedily ingested the
doctrine that declares that there is no value

anointed to an earnest effort if there is no
moneyed endorsement fastened to its face, no

alabaster hands handling the sealed deal, the
counting of the value declared by the valuable. Does

it count that I can speak the language of the colonizer
with my Negro pen while holding fast to my soul?

Unbought and unbossed makes equal sense within a
dissolving marketplace of the imagination when

everywhere we are hangs a noose for our collective
capture. The creator and the consumer in fetal

combat, monitored by capitalist teets tightly
manufacturing salience through clicks and likes,

always profiting off of our moral outrage, always
deeming us illegitimate until none of this counts.

None of this matters. So, I write praisesongs for the
writer who writes even when she is without patron,

without a promise land in the form of an advance and
an agent. Praises to her clever copyright, her LLC

and her annual gofundme. Blessings over her sidewalk
readings and car trunk sales, praises to her

sweaty brow under the tent where she sits and sells
her books on Juneteenth. Praises to antiperspirant

that doesn't leave white marks on these particularly
hot days that remind her that yes, she is a writer. Yes,

her work matters. Praisesong for the job that she holds
on to fund this writing life and all the things she

does creatively. I am only able to be her on the days I
believe that I am a writer and I am real, too.

PART II:

Memories That Feel Like Milestones

Grill Cheese, Please

It's the crisp for me, the way the cheese lets the bread
get a word in, cracking its crinkled brown face

in exhale, because everybody knows butter makes
white bread turn Black. And, my granddaddy's grill

cheese was hella Black, tasting like summer and porch
laughs, ashy knees rubbed down with some

cocoa butter after five hours of swimming in the hot
sun. At my grandaddy's house, Black folks swam, got

our hair wet and played in the heat, even if my
grandmama didn't sit out there with us too long. "I got

my big hat for that," she always say. PaPa would
always mention he had some frozen pizzas we liked

or he could make some grilled cheese for lunch when
we went back to he and MaMa's condo after

swimming at the complex pool since 9am. My reply
was always, "Grill Cheese, please." I used to live

with MaMa and PaPa with my mother when I was
younger and they were still in their house on Taylor

street in DC. Mommy said they sold the house
because PaPa was getting too old to take care of all

the things the house needed. The condo is smaller
than the first floor of their old house. But, the grilled

cheese still tastes warm and comfortable. With my
teeth breaking through the final tear of crust, licking

the last languid drip of melting American cheese
before it drops on my bathing suit, I am already full.

Seeing My Reflection

Casting a dripping reflection,
It's a long deep
Going
A leap within the interior
of this slipping mask
A peeping echo that calls its own name,
In it, eyes sip infinity

My First Tattoo

got my first tattoo
five days ago
on a thursday,
the day after
turning 51

i had said before
that i would
never
get a tattoo
because i can't
imagine
having someone
draw something
on me
permanently
&having to wear
that for the
rest of my life

but, today,
i figure, i
got more
years behind
me than ahead
&i love the sun
& the moon
& i come from the stars,
so if i draw

them on my arm,
maybe i get
to go home
sooner or
at least feel like
i'm there already
every time i look down

Revisionist Tale

i pick up and put away fallen toys and random pieces of clothes and imagine my life before/ before when floors were bare and so was the refrigerator and there was no rush to fill it nor prepare dinner because "who eats?" on Fridays anyway, not me & i exhale/winded after constant bending and rising, straightening items that stand less than four feet tall, preparing to vacuum. in amazement that in a four year-span brown can become gray and worries change in chameleon fashion from single and dating to play dates and naps/ quiet time alone, now, a coveted reward instead of an unwanted declaration./ i replace markers to their bins, dolls to their perches and dress-up clothes to their closet/ closing the door, i remember unfinished tasks that await and consume the silence in thirsty gratefulness, undaunted by her impending arrival.

Little Purse

i used to carry
 my sweet little baby
with me everywhere i went
like a   little purse
i would wear her
 in scarves &african printed
 cloth& headwraps turned into
slings &i would
carry her to work
  &to the market &
to the park
&to the end of the street
&back
then
she held my everything
   in her little being
like ambitions&reveries
&better-than-now
i just wanted her to have eternity
& so when
she began traipsing
on her round brown toes
i'd fill her
   head of crinkly curls
w/ unicorn thoughts
&amethyst intentions
holding her small hand
 ambling here

&there
as we haunted theatres
&museums
&concerts
&faraway golden places
 as she sprouted&tblossomed
getting taller &brighter than the sun
&writing her own
        musings into well-worn journals

she now carries in her own   little purse

A Careful Grooming

I remember that
I only once before was I unguarded.
I'd often miss the
big things. Always, it is
the small things I see.

My name
is not sweetness
in his mouth, I
remember thinking.
During class, it does not
slide smooth
Nor bring smiles
to each corner. It
sits dry and stale
alone at the tip
of his acrid tongue. Angry
at its exile.

But, now, outside,
he coughs
it earnestly,
pretends an ease
he does not seem
to believe.
I did not realize then
his wish to devour
was insatiable.
He packaged casualness

within playful banter
and interest in my writing.
This attention
cornered my fascination
in its greedy snare.
At 21, I am a lion's prey.

A grey-flecked, whiskered man,
he must have seen his yesteryear
reflected in my eyes,
cradling his arrogance
as a stately trophy.
His approach was
hesitant and ambitious,
betrayed by deep craving
for softness
and forgiveness.

I was a fountain
that flows and forgets.

I am, now, a river of never endings.

The Dating Game in 1996

I hate it
Sparsely furnished and dimly lit--your apartment reeks
from male pomposity and arbitrary attitude
dark leather sofa, bookcase-less collections,
forgotten framed prints leaning against the wall
I stagger
Overcome by the bleakness of non-commitment
weighed down by the stench of gigolo-itis
if only you'd make your bed
I'd stay

swish swat (or another name for the subplot in 90% of Tyler Perry movies)

I.

he   speaks liquid words slipping easily
into your youthful   bloom
      winged archers   circling
rounding the blushing prey   a hunt for pretty smells
delicious   tastes like drops of chocolate   on your
tongue
  melting smoothness that disappears
you forget your quiet you forget your no's and can't
do's
   you forgettttt as you slide towards his grinning
charm

II.

you only fanning now
'cuz your hands can't keep still
you ain't hot. you mad.   at yourself.
you swish&swat back and forth
 in time to your rising foul mood.
didn't nobody tell you to relax.   you s'posed to stay
on guard.
why you believe him
when he said you pretty?
you think your pretty is worth
more than his satin mouth
filled with soft words that

push deeper inside you than his hard thickness?
girl, his life depends on the honey of your yes.

III.

if she knew that she was the blossom born from a
predator's kiss,
would her life become a shriek of joy or sadness?
is his dna a jerky scab on her mitochondria? will it
matter?
you will spend your life scrubbing his oiliness from your
skin.
but, your motherly pretend will not erase his imprint
from
her bones

The Good in Goodbye

A leaving treads well
when it follows closely to
the will of the soul

Why We Celebrate Poets

Poets are our culture keepers
Wearing the elements of each feeling they encounter,
Poets code switch between the dialect of the mystic
and the commoner
Twirling consonants and vowels into a magical brew

Turning the chaos of emotions into docile fluidity
For a reader or listener to greedily savor
Poets document each moment with a sculptor's
precision,
Arranging words into communal memory

Slicking soft the ragged edges of trauma and cruelty,
Decorating the moments of joy and recovery
Poets greet our senses with lingering familiarity.
The beings who hold the poet's spirit within are our
community's soul.

They feel the sounds, taste the textures,
Hear the colors and witness the loudness
And quiet of each corner of humanity.
They bear the humility of our failings

And the laughter of our triumphs,
Sweeping the crevices of the mundane
To find the treasured moments that matter.
The cellular root of our culture's blood are our poets, in
motion,

Witnessing the whirling wonder of our future,
Our present, our past,
Their decoded messages live forever
Beyond their breath.

These Jobs

(Written for the Winter 2024 UMBC graduating class)

And what about these jobs, you ask?
How do we find them? How do we determine they are
a fit?

How do we know we have found a place,
worthy of our joy and excitement?

How do we understand what is compatible for a long
or short stay?
Do we dismiss an offer immediately or accept it with
dismay?

What about these jobs, you ask?
The ones we worked so hard to get.

The ones we prepared ourselves to be chosen for,
sometimes with very little discernment.

The jobs that make us make a decision
between our mental health and a decent pay,

The ones who work us unmercifully,
 family time always on delay.

What about these jobs, you ask?
What about these careers?

What about this work you
have been studying for years upon years?

How do you make it matter?
How do you decide on what to show care?

How do you create something
out of the nothing that is there?

The answer is the question is the journey, is the find.
The answer is in your habits, in your beliefs, and in your
mind.

The answer relies on your values,
your decisions and your ideas on your self-worth.

The answer is in what ideas
you nurture, then implement, and give birth.
In our power is the agency
to make a choice on where we land.

We have the tools to make space for the skills
we have developed and the knowledge we
understand.

We are within this period of time
where others will tell us where to go and what to do.

But no one knows what is your best route,
because no one else is you.

What about these jobs you ask?
What next must you do?

My advice is to make the decision to know your mind.
Know your own heart and stay true to your vision for
you.

Your next step in your journey is a quest to impact
this world, this nation, or your local community.

Your next step will be a testament
to what you learned while earning your degree.

Your learning will continue despite you leaving the
walls of a classroom.
The world will become your learning lab, whether in
real time or on a zoom.

You will be tested to deliver your best or worst version
of yourself.
You will be given options, choosing between integrity
or bundles of hoarded wealth.

These jobs will not be the defining factor of all you
have become.
It will ultimately be based on your interior self and the
moral compass you lead from.

What about these jobs, my friend?
What is next for you?

All that I ask is
to thine own self be true.

Making

I am softened leather,
tendered by the beatings
by the years
as I am
Making more of me
to come,
Ready for the turning
of the hands

I make dinner
from the separate shelves
that host potatoes
and shriveled bell peppers
as welcomed guests

Throw them
in a pot
to dance happily
as they are roasted unmercifully

I meal on their death

Wishes
landing carefully
on sparse clouds
promising rain,
synching vibrations
that heal and harm

A contradiction

I dreamed
I was salvation,
perfectly content
as I make destruction
my lethal friend

the choice is yours

you can get with this or you can get with that,
a muting of your soul,
a check that's pretty phat,
if truth be really told,
it all is pretty wack,
ain't nothing worth the price,
of selling off your Black

The Offering

I offered my seat
and they sat.
Said friends
were coming.

I moved
to another seat.
Still at the table. Their
friends arrived.
Took up
all the open seats.

I had some things
on the table.
Wrapped my arms
around them things
and pulled them
closer to me. Offered
to share. They grabbed

and pulled and
snatched before the offer
finished leaving my
lips. Left me with not much.

Didn't offer me nothing
of their stuff. But, I took
some anyway. Took some
of this. Some of that. A

little of that. Still carry
some of this in my purse.

The table, after all, was
mine first.

Immodesty

the old folks
will tell you that
it is to humble you,
to make sure you

don't forget your
beginnings. ur
friends will agree.
they remind you to

not get too big.
stay small. not enough
skimpy air to share, they say.
sometimes. most times,

they will say nothing.
pretend to not take notice.
whispers that eye and ogle.
wordless attention that

changes the subject.
their envy prays for a
falling, an avalanche that will unalive
all of the seedlings you have

planted. they don't know yet
that you are a deep rooting,
a vining thunder. a swirling dream.
This Now is only

The beginning.

When Do We Get Up?

How do we get up
when the ceiling is falling
and the rent is due?

When the world is spinning
at phantom velocity
And the faces around you
sneer venom as ritual,

Why would you get up?

You get up because
this is your world, too
This is your space
and place to imagine
your wildest dreams
and bring them to fruition

You are light and depth
and the muse's best gift

Don't you know your name?

A wakening is in your belly
that puts your inhibitions
to shame and shallows
your transgressions

This right here
is when all your talents
are unfolded
and shared with the world

We need you!

The thinkers,
the carers,
the world whisperers
who remember our original names

The ones with wooden feet
that catch fire and turn to wings
Carrying our messages to the sky

Branding the stars
with our jazz and sacred geometry
Kissing the comets
with sonnets of wisdom's divine plan

We need you!

The brave ones
who pound the pavement
with such durable resistance

The careful ones
who read between the lines
The thoughtful ones
who are forever protecting,
forever sharing,
forever loving us

We become a better world
when we remember all of the power
that co-exists within our veins,
intermixing with the mitochondrial memories
of our complicated past

Your voice is crystal
Your heart is a fluid river
Your courage to speak truth to power

And call a thing a thing is your greatest work of art.

Staring at Trees Out of a Dirty Window

my bones
sink deeper
into the mattress
despite
the shriek of my phone's
bugle call. the sky
snores exhale
gray. it looks
like it may snow
or rain,
morning sun
still asleep,
hidden
behind tree
branches
bent like broken
backs of dying
dandelions. it is
december's quiet
chill that has
chased the birds
away,
leaving the
tremble of traffic
as its only
audio
for this early hours
visual. a splotchy
unclean

window panel
merges
with the rising
smoke leaving
my neighbor's chimney.
i prepare to
move, too

Summer 2024 Prediction

Sweltering heat mewls
like a kitten, air thickly
brimming steam vapor

the girl who spoke to the universe

there was a little girl who was alone in front of the window looking outside wondering, "what was there to life," and "what was life there?" "where did things begin?" "where do things become and how did creation create itself?"

this little girl wondered about oblivion and all of the things that lived outside of the window, and far beyond the sky's blue. the little girl who was alone began to go inside herself to find the parts that could explain the why's, the who's, the hows, and the..."where was her mother?" she often wondered why her mother was always so invisible. the universe would reply most times with answers found painted on a sun ray, seen in a reflection shining in the window, or heard in a songbird's wail.

walls failed to keep the girl small. she grew tall on a diet of books that she ate for breakfast. she gulped words that sounded like silk, tangled in her mouth. she was a grateful lover of the tranquility that reading bestowed, silently guiding her trailing fingers across each page, occasionally whispering consonants that danced on her tongue. she was a ravenous devourer of language, a burgeoning beacon of brilliance.

she grew as tall as each story she read. her curls grew longer, her imagination expanded as she became close kin with each character in each book introduced to her. plaiting Anne of Green Gables' red braids,

solving mysteries with Nancy Drew who was
brown-sknned in her mind's eye, she loved Terabithia
as her own special kingdom. closing the books
became harder each time.

the little girl was now a sprouting beanstalk with a
blossoming thirst for the world around her. she had
become a maker of poems, a weaver of her own
short stories as her world slowly began to narrow in
and words bubbled everywhere, not just in books.
even under water, the words still found her
(sometimes with their own soundtrack). the curtains
blowing in the wind hummed melodies she could write
songs to. years later she will remember that even this
early, she was already a playwright, too.

the little girl twirls into adulthood, unprepared for the
expectation that she is to hand over her imagination in
exchange for job security and credentials, a paycheck
and a home. the language that had been her closest
confidante prepared to mildew in its loneliness as it
watched her unfasten her magic from her hair,
reducing herself to silence as she looked tentatively
around, as if hiding something. trembling, the words
were fearful she would soon disappear, unable to be
saved. until. sensing their heightened angst, she turned
to them, finger to lips with a hushing smile, pointing to
the wings, hidden beneath her hem, still fastened at
her feet.

PART III:

Affirmations & Toasts To and From the Ancestors

seedling

I grow when
love waters drench me

in yes and
let's go and do this

and try this
and think about this

because.
because we can
because we are here
because we are here now, today

while I am seed young,
watered by free and truth,

blossoming into beginning that
spirals Fibonacci,

planting thoughts eternal,
monogrammed in helix shape,

blooming possibility,
in hieroglyphic shapeshifting, saturated in

crescent moon tide energy.
I grow when love is infinity,

turning back to begin again.
understanding

the journey is the reason,
never the end.

Relief

When women dance,
the world exhales.
Fumes of relief
For she now knows peace.

seeds of the middle passage (pt.2)

Trapped in the wobbly full belly of a ship prison
Brimming with misery
My great-great-great-great-great-great
grandmother chose to breathe
Forgiving God, she clung to living—inhaling, exhaling
Imprinting DNA with remembrance,
Blood cell memory instructed to carry on
Trauma imprints don't fade
Even after the brain decides to forget
Wrestling with living demons
She chose to live

June's Teeth

June's teeth got a hold of us,
the month of Father's Day,
Black Music month,
and LGBT Pride,

June 19th sits respectfully
wearing red, white and blue
within the center of its mouth,
quietly inside. Dixie's wallflower.

Jubilee brews, folks get ready
dancing and singing aloud,
deep baritone seeping through
the center of June's teeth. June 19th

stays sitting proud. She can recite the
long struggles of the descendants
of enslaved women and men.
Communes with their ghosts,

cries their tears so they can sleep.
And, we give praise. We channel the ancestors
who we will never know. Whisper thanks as
we embrace each tender relic of our stolen history.

June 19th guarded the hearth. Sat at the feet
of our truth tellers as the colonizers threatened to
lure her away. But, one day, her fingers pulled from
ours.
Accepted their trinkets and wiles. Forgetting,
forgetting

the people who lived before,
our dear ancestors brought to this country

to be bought and sold
Within the teeth of June.

June 19th begins to forget that our walk
towards true liberation has only just begun
She climbs into the mouth and the belly
of the beast, donning the costume of the con.

She is now willing tool of propaganda, a Trojan
Horse cracking through the door. Branding t-shirts
with her broken smile. The 19th sashays cheaply,
now only a trivial day of of remembrance,

carrying discounted tickets to the club,
wrapping a burning flag around her body twice.
June's teeth are sharpened steel. An insistent
menace, a day off from work.

Unified Sankofa

We form circle
in communal silence
Heads bowed, lips still

a collective rewinding
with each beat of the drum,
always the drum, speaking

Back Back Back Back   Back Back
BackBack Back BackBack Back
Back ah Back Back Back ah Back Back

as Spirits chant solemnly
from the sidelines waving
the fumes of the past moving towards us

Back Back Back Back   Back Back
BackBack Back BackBack Back
Back ah Back Back Back ah Back Back

We see infinity
within each artery,
Our cells' nucleus holding treasure

Great Grandmother, I see you
Grandmother, I hear you
Mother, I feel you here, right here!

Back Back Back Back   Back Back
BackBack Back BackBack Back
Back ah Back Back Back ah Back Back

I am encoded, I am a vessel
carrying within me
my whole village

I am the village
that holds my daughter's
sons and daughters

Back Back Back Back   Back Back
BackBack Back BackBack Back
Back ah Back Back Back ah Back Back

clearing the air for their arrival,
planting the seeds for their survival,
writing the recipes

holding fast to our remnants
that have struggled to survive,
within me, they are still alive

We are Haptepshut,
DuSable, Kemet before the rewrite,
We are. We are We are.

We form circle
We remember
looking back

with wonder and chagrin
In unified mission we understand our past
Before the order of today can begin

Black is

Heat
That heavy *hot hot* when
we clapping and singing and stomping
and shouting, holding up to the heavens our heaviest
burdens

Thankful and forgiving
A warming that is fueled by our gathering

Black is
A Feast
Whether Easter or Christmas, Thanksgiving or New
Year's,
a birthday or a funeral, a nourishing is prepared
Pilot-fire lit upon arrival, welcomed into tight hugs
into waiting bosoms,
fist bumps and back pats,
stirred into sticky cornbread batter and simmering
greens

Black is
A colorful cultivating
A cultural crescendo
A determined declaration
A powerful pushback
A "no" to a rising tide of indifference and violence
A blossoming of a bud from the center of cracked
consent

Black is
An unwillingness to bend
To defeat
To dehumanization
To a terminal displacement

that clings and smothers

Black is
a candle of remembrance
a circling of bowed heads
and clasped hands
is ancestors in
calling calling calling out to you
Don't you forget yourself, don't you forget your people,
don't you forget your path!

Oh, this path!

Black is
This path
This walk
This heavy, humbling, steady walk
This mighty, rousing, staggering walk,
This Malcolm, Martin, Ella walk

Black is
This laugh
This cry
These hands

Black is our babies
Is our future
Is this present
Is this us

Black is
This life

Black is

Hands

These hands
These hands

Shake hands
Pat shoulders

Squeeze arms
Prayyyyyyy

Prayyyyyyy

These hands
Light candles

Stir things
Blow kisses

Wave goodbye
Wave hello

Point there
And there

And here,
These hands

Write poems
And songs

Pass out flyers
And books

"Read this!"
These hands

Pinch fat cheeks
Burp babies

Build sand castles
Throw snowballs

These hands
These hands

Beat a djembe drum
Hold a microphone

Pour a glass of wine
Caress my lover

Gently

These hands
Are gentle

Are soft
Are rough

Are fists
Are slapping hands

Are righteous hands
Are upward
Don't shoot
Don't shoot

"Stop!"

Are fists
Black Power

These hands
Strike "No!"

Push enemies away
Pull kindred closer

Punch and crack glass ceilings
These hands

These hands
These hands

These hands
Hold it together

Hold weeping heads
These hands

Wipe tears
These hands are knocking

Knocking on your window

Yoohoo! Are you sleeping?

Do you see this?
Do you see this?

These hands
Hold things

Wear rings that tell stories
These hands

Were smooth once
Were soft

Were empty
These hands

With veins and lines
With bone and skin

Push dying grandfathers in wheelchairs
Help grandmothers to their feet

Lift gurgling infants to the sky
Lay a flower on the chest of mother in a coffin

These hands
Hold pain

and laughter
Hold memories

hold it together
Hold it together

Hold the hurt
Hold typing fingers

That are typing this poem
Are remembering each story

They hold
These hands

Hold them
Hold these hands

These hands hold stories
These hands

These hands
These hands

We Need Each Other

Our differences are the patterns
we wear like rainbows in the night.
Our similarities are abundant, hidden in plain sight.

We are in need of each other
But sometimes don't realize
how much until it is too late.

We confuse the idea of community
(with a striving for individualism)
until we encounter one another and can't relate.

We are in need of each other
but sometimes don't understand
what that really means.

We only seek out other people
when preoccupied with
our own hopes and dreams.

We are on this human journey
as spiritual beings
trying to understand who we are.

We have forgotten that we each hold the power
to radically change this world,
made from the carbon of fallen stars.

We are in need of each other.
We are the connecting piece
to make this world make sense.

We help each other

with understanding,
when the noise around us becomes too dense.

We need each other
so that we can remember
the depths from which we have crawled.

We need each other
to decipher the meaning
on the walls of time where our history is scrawled.

Embrace the sacredness
of our connectivity,
and the reasons for which we are alive.

We need each other
Each sister and brother,
If we wish to continue to survive.

Our differences are the patterns
we wear like rainbows in the night.
Our similarities are abundant, hidden in plain sight.

Final Destination

We stand on the precipice
where love is struggling to call our name
Catching its breath from the tsunami
of chaos and evergreen untruth
That swirls in never-ending struggle

But, it is our birthright to clamor to its side,
and become courage
(be brave, be strong, be strength)

Pick up its torch of unending light
that is the portal to all that is knowing
(we are the light.)

And softness (and resilience)
And peace (and determination)
And joy (and joy)
Oh, joy,

What a dark hour we find ourselves,
but, with love, you are our final destination
(our guiding star)

Clutching us closer
to each moment
(we are ready.)

Brimming with new promise
of a fresh start

(a new beginning)

Where hatred has
no space to breathe
(no place to roam)

Where barbaric indifference
to humanity has no roots to plant
We stand on the precipice
where love is calling
(is calling to you)

Where love is growing
(growing to the heavens above)

Where love is taking over and
Stamping this moment as its own
(a better place, a better day, for you and me)

The Swell

Rushing, coursing eagerly in anticipation
Toward a moment
Where evaporation is inevitable.

But, oh how glorious it is to be
A blessing.
Salvation
To the dry, cracked, empty and desolate
Of mind, heart & spirit
Until you are absorbed.

Your essence hydration.
As rain,
you are eternal.

BLACK PEOPLE

Black people

hold your head high, don't you falter when you speak
showcase the strength of your mind, body and soul
you are not lazy, passive or weak

You have been sold a false hood about who you are
And who you can potentially become
You have had the truth of your lineage be mishandled
through misinformation
Until you are not clear about the greatness from which
you have sprung

Black people

Get your house in order, step into your power as
strong women and men
Protect your peace as you protect your home
Cultivating truth, respect, discipline and wisdom

Tap into the energy of the universe
The sacred geometry of all living things
The medicine in nature at our fingertips
The calmness that true power brings

Black people

Go about forgetting the lies
that have been told repeatedly to you
About what success is, what the American Dream is
and all the things you know are not true

Become acquainted once again
with the land you stand upon

Dispel the myths of the "forefathers"
and tall tales that have been spun

Kneel into the soil, touch the trees
and laugh with the plants and flowers
Find your breath, and connect with your inner self
before you reach your final hour

Black people

Most of all, find your place
here in this world
Magnify your greatness by leading by example
for each of our young boys and girls
Use your time wisely my friends,
don't delay in taking advantage of time
For it moves quicker, not slower,
and is gone before you realize

Black people

I wish you love,
I send you grace
and pray for protection over your words,
your minds, your bodies and your hearts.

May you have lives
that reflect the masterpiece of your design,
as you are a living
and breathing work of art

Ashe

Soothe/Say

i predicted
this moment
when i was reborn without language and empathy,

when i was babble
and bluster,
shaky legs and watching
eyes with fists clutched tight

i predicted this collapse.
unsettled by my return
to a sour world
steeped in in-ordinary
violence,

i remembered this place,
mind tumbling
To forget

the repetitive accuracy
is a long-stemmed rose
blooming with thorns poised to prick

each time, my death
comes in the morning, an extinguished exhale through
rotten debris

holding up hands to catch
the light, to be the light
exclaim ruffled words

that only plead for empty time

this is where they co-opt
your pain
swallow your screams
bathe in your black rock
misery before memorizing
the fine lines etched within
your broken spirit
renaming this new discovery
as something other than your own,
they make a necklace of your hope to circle their
ghoulish throat

this reunion is their last attempt to defile the shadows
that will not die

this is our final incarnation to dispel the ash of their
envy and blow the dust from our own eyes before we
are doomed to reenter this world that crumbles where
we stand

Your Final Instructions Before Fully Shining Your Light and Stepping Into Your Future

Remember this moment. Imprint in your
mind the roundness of this day, its ridged
shape that has brought news that offers
a passport to your future.

Count the smiles, laughs, cheers
and amens from the loved ones who are
clapping for you. Tuck that number close
to your heart and count it softly.

They are your angels. Most of them will meet you
at the finish line. Some may take flight during
your journey and become your celestial
protectors. All of them are loving you madly right now.

And, it is for them, maybe, that you studied
so hard and climbed so far to memorize, recite
and test your way to your next stage, but this
next stop will be about you.

What is in your heart, your mind, your spirit?

What lingers in your soul's deepest caverns
that speaks to the embers that become
your inner flame? What spurs you to imagine,
create, inspire and lead?

Who are you when no one is looking?

This next step is your opportunity to meet yourself in
your barest moments, where there is no reminder to
speak well, wake up, dress nicely, treat others with
dignity and respect. Each interaction from here on out
will be perfectly constructed by you.

Who are you when no one is watching?
Are you kindness? Are you ambition?
Are you medicine for a wound that is this world?
You will soon become familiar with the you that lives
within,

The one who may be sleeping or yawning or wide
awake, eager to burst into the light. Just remember,
that with great privilege comes great responsibility
and it is your debt to yourself to choose wisely the next
steps you make into the world.

For, the world, in all of its messy joys, darkest horrors,
epic beauty and perfect quiet has been spinning
patiently, rotating off of its predictable route, requiring
from you the brilliant

attention that only you can give.

All that it asks is that
You Keep Going,
Keep Glowing, Forever Shining
Your Ever Bright Light.

Learn more about Khadijah Z. Ali-Coleman by visiting
KhadijahAli-Coleman.com

Learn more about
Black Writers for Peace and Social Justice, Inc. by
visiting BlackWritersforPeace.org

Black Writers for Peace and Social Justice (BWPSJ) is a
501(c)3 nonprofit organization providing skill-building
learning experiences and opportunities for Black
writers and offering administrative training and
services for literary and community-based
organizations intent on public engagement practice
founded in tenets of peace and social justice.

We envision a world where stories are tools for
liberation, the arts are central to social justice
movements, and diverse voices lead the way toward
understanding, empathy, justice, and equity.

www.ingramcontent.com/pod-product-compliance
Lightning Source LLC
Chambersburg PA
CBHW061241140726
47998CB00006B/2059